Contents

CW00410874

Section 1: Introduction

What is an Approved Document?

1.1 This Approved Document, which takes effect on 1 October 2010, has been approved and issued by the Secretary of State to provide practical guidance on ways of complying with the **energy efficiency requirements** (see Section 2) and regulation 7 of the Building Regulations 2000 (SI 2000/2531) for England and Wales, as amended. Regulation 2(1) of the Building Regulations defines the **energy efficiency requirements** as the requirements of regulations 4A, 17C, 17D and 17E and Part L of Schedule 1. The Building Regulations 2000 are referred to throughout the remainder of this Document as 'the Building Regulations'.

1.2 The intention of issuing Approved Documents is to provide guidance about compliance with specific aspects of building regulations in some of the more common building situations. They set out what, in ordinary circumstances, may be accepted as reasonable provision for compliance with the relevant requirement(s) of building regulations to which they refer.

1.3 If guidance in an Approved Document is followed there will be a presumption of compliance with the requirement(s) covered by the guidance. However, this presumption can be overturned, so simply following guidance does not guarantee compliance; for example, if the particular case is unusual in some way, then 'normal' guidance may not be applicable. It is also important to note that there may well be other ways of achieving compliance with the requirements. **There is therefore no obligation to adopt any particular solution contained in this Approved Document if you would prefer to meet the relevant requirement in some other way. Persons intending to carry out building work should always check with their building control body, either the local authority or an approved inspector, that their proposals comply with building regulations.**

1.4 It is important to note that this Approved Document, as well as containing guidance, also contains extracts from the Regulations. Such regulatory text must be complied with as stated. For example, the requirement that the target CO_2 emission rate for the building shall not be exceeded (regulation 17C) is a regulatory requirement. There is therefore no flexibility to ignore this requirement; neither can compliance with this particular regulation be demonstrated via any route other than that set out in regulations 17A and 17B.

1.5 The guidance contained in this Approved Document relates only to the particular requirements of the Building Regulations that the document addresses (set out in Section 2). However, building work may be subject to more than one requirement of building regulations. In such cases the work will also have to comply with any other applicable building regulations.

1.6 There are Approved Documents that give guidance on each of the Parts of Schedule 1 and on regulation 7. A full list of these is provided at the back of this document.

Consideration of technical risk

1.7 In relation to the construction of new buildings other than **dwellings**, building work must satisfy all the technical requirements set out in regulations 17C and 17E of, and Schedule 1 to, the Building Regulations. When considering the incorporation of energy efficiency measures in **dwellings**, attention should be paid in particular to the need to comply with Part B (fire safety), Part C (site preparation and resistance to contaminants and moisture), Part E (resistance to the passage of sound), Part F (ventilation), Paragraph G3 (hot water storage), Part J (combustion appliances and fuel storage systems) and Part P (electrical safety), as well as Part L. The adoption of any particular energy efficiency measure should not involve unacceptable technical risk of, for instance, excessive condensation. Designers and builders should refer to the relevant Approved Documents and to other generally available good practice guidance to help minimise these risks.

How to use this Approved Document

1.8 This Approved Document is subdivided into seven sections as detailed below. These main sections are followed by supporting appendices.

This **introductory** section sets out the general context in which the guidance in the Approved Documents must be considered.

Section 2 sets out the relevant legal requirements as published in the Building Regulations.

Section 3 contains general guidance, including the definition of key terms, the types of building work covered by this Approved Document, the types of building work that are exempt, procedures for notifying work, materials and workmanship and health and safety issues, an overview of the routes to compliance and how to deal with 'special' areas of buildings that contain **dwellings**.

Section 4 details the considerations that apply to demonstrating that the design of the building will meet the **energy efficiency requirements**. This section begins the detailed technical guidance relating to showing compliance with the **energy efficiency requirements**.

Section 5 details the considerations that apply when demonstrating that the design has been appropriately translated into actual construction performance.

Section 6 describes the information that should be provided to occupiers to help them achieve reasonable standards of energy efficiency in practice.

Section 7 provides a pointer to some useful information on different design approaches to meeting the *energy efficiency requirements*.

1.9   In this document the following conventions have been adopted to assist understanding and interpretation:

a. Texts shown against a green background are extracts from the Building Regulations or Building (Approved Inspectors etc.) Regulations 2000 (SI 2000/2532) ('the Approved Inspectors Regulations'), both as amended, and set out the legal requirements that relate to compliance with the *energy efficiency requirements* of building regulations. As stated previously, there is no flexibility in respect of such text; it defines a legal requirement, not guidance for typical situations. It should also be remembered that, as noted above, building works must comply with all the other applicable provisions of building regulations.

b. Key terms are defined in paragraph 3.1 and are printed in *bold italic text*.

c. Details of technical publications referred to in the text of this Approved Document will be given in footnotes and repeated as references at the end of the document. A reference to a publication is likely to be made for one of two main reasons. The publication may contain additional or more comprehensive technical detail, which it would be impractical to include in full in the document but which is needed to fully explain ways of meeting the requirements; or it is a source of more general information. The reason for the reference will be indicated in each case. The reference will be to a specified edition of the document. The Approved Document may be amended from time to time to include new references or to refer to revised editions where this aids compliance.

d. Additional *commentary in italic text* appears after some numbered paragraphs. This commentary is intended to assist understanding of the immediately preceding paragraph or sub-paragraph, or to direct readers to sources of additional information, but is not part of the technical guidance itself.

Where you can get further help

1.10   If you do not understand the technical guidance or other information set out in this Approved Document and the additional detailed technical references to which it directs you, there are a number of routes through which you can seek further assistance:

*   the CLG website: www.communities.gov.uk;

*   the Planning Portal website: www.planningportal.gov.uk;

*   if you are the person undertaking the building work you can seek assistance either from your local authority building control service or from your approved inspector (depending on which building control service you are using);

*   persons registered with a competent person self-certification scheme may be able to get technical advice from their scheme operator;

*   if your query is of a highly technical nature you may wish to seek the advice of a specialist, or industry technical body, in the area of concern.

Responsibility for compliance

1.11   It is important to remember that if you are the person (e.g. designer, builder, installer) carrying out building work to which any requirement of building regulations applies you have a responsibility to ensure that the work complies with any such requirement. The building owner may also have a responsibility for ensuring compliance with building regulation requirements and could be served with an enforcement notice in cases of non-compliance.

Section 2: The Requirements

2.1 This Approved Document, which takes effect on 1 October 2010, deals with the **energy efficiency requirements** in the Building Regulations 2000 (as amended). Regulation 2(1) of the Building Regulations defines the **energy efficiency requirements** as the requirements of regulations 4A, 17C, 17D and 17E and Part L of Schedule 1. The **energy efficiency requirements** relevant to this Approved Document, which deals with new buildings other than **dwellings**, are those in regulations 17C and 17E and Part L of Schedule 1, and are set out below.

New buildings – Regulation 17C

Where a building is erected, it shall not exceed the target CO_2 emission rate for the building that has been approved pursuant to regulation 17B.

Energy performance certificates – Regulation 17E

(1) This regulation applies where–

(a) a building is erected; or

(b) a building is modified so that it has a greater or fewer number of parts designed or altered for separate use than it previously had, where the modification includes the provision or extension of any of the fixed services for heating, hot water, air conditioning or mechanical ventilation.

(2) The person carrying out the work shall–

(a) give an energy performance certificate for the building to the owner of the building; and

(b) give to the local authority notice to that effect, including the reference number under which the energy performance certificate has been registered in accordance with regulation 17F(4).

(3) The energy performance certificate and notice shall be given not later than five days after the work has been completed.

(4) The energy performance certificate must be accompanied by a recommendation report containing recommendations for the improvement of the energy performance of the building, issued by the energy assessor who issued the energy performance certificate.

(5) An energy performance certificate must–

(a) express the asset rating of the building in a way approved by the Secretary of State under regulation 17A;

(b) include a reference value such as a current legal standard or benchmark;

(c) be issued by an energy assessor who is accredited to produce energy performance certificates for that category of building; and

---

Energy performance certificates – Regulation 17E *(continued)*

(d) include the following information–

(i) the reference number under which the certificate has been registered in accordance with regulation 17F(4);

(ii) the address of the building;

(iii) an estimate of the total useful floor area of the building;

(iv) the name of the energy assessor who issued it;

(v) the name and address of the energy assessor's employer, or, if he is self-employed, the name under which he trades and his address;

(vi) the date on which it was issued; and

(vii) the name of the approved accreditation scheme of which the energy assessor is a member.

(6) Certification for apartments or units designed or altered for separate use in blocks may be based–

(a) except in the case of a dwelling, on a common certification of the whole building for blocks with a common heating system; or

(b) on the assessment of another representative apartment or unit in the same block.

(7) Where–

(a) a block with a common heating system is divided into parts designed or altered for separate use; and

(b) one or more, but not all, of the parts are dwellings,

certification for those parts which are not dwellings may be based on a common certification of all the parts which are not dwellings.

Requirement	*Limits on application*

Schedule 1 – Part L Conservation of fuel and power

L1. Reasonable provision shall be made for the conservation of fuel and power in buildings by:

(a) limiting heat gains and losses–

(i) through thermal elements and other parts of the building fabric; and

(ii) from pipes, ducts and vessels used for space heating, space cooling and hot water services;

(b) providing fixed building services which–

(i) are energy efficient;

(ii) have effective controls; and

(iii) are commissioned by testing and adjusting as necessary to ensure they use no more fuel and power than is reasonable in the circumstances; and

(c) providing to the owner sufficient information about the building, the fixed building services and their maintenance requirements so that the building can be operated in such a manner as to use no more fuel and power than is reasonable in the circumstances.

LIMITATION ON REQUIREMENTS

2.2   In accordance with regulation 8 of the Building Regulations, the requirements in Parts A to D, F to K and N and P (except for paragraphs G2, H2 and J6) of Schedule 1 to the Building Regulations do not require anything to be done except for the purpose of securing reasonable standards of health and safety for persons in or about buildings (and any others who may be affected by buildings or matters connected with buildings).

2.3   Paragraph G2 is excluded as it deals with water efficiency and paragraphs H2 and J6 are excluded from regulation 8 because they deal directly with prevention of the contamination of water. Parts E and M (which deal, respectively, with resistance to the passage of sound, and access to and use of buildings) are excluded from regulation 8 because they address the welfare and convenience of building users. Part L is excluded from regulation 8 because it addresses the conservation of fuel and power.

Section 3: General guidance

Key terms

3.1 The following are key terms used in this document:

Air permeability is the physical property used to measure airtightness of the building fabric. It is defined as air leakage rate per hour per square metre of envelope area at the test reference pressure differential across the building envelope of 50 Pascal (50 N/m²). The envelope area of the building, or measured part of the building, is the total area of all floors, walls and ceilings bordering the internal volume subject to the test. This includes walls and floors below external ground level. Overall internal dimensions are used to calculate this area and no subtractions are made for the area of the junctions of internal walls, floors and ceilings with exterior walls, floors and ceilings. The *limiting air permeability* is the worst allowable *air permeability*. The *design air permeability* is the target value set at the design stage, and must always be no worse than the limiting value. The *assessed air permeability* is the value used in establishing the *BER*, and is based on a specific measurement of the building concerned.

BCB means Building Control Body: a local authority or an approved inspector.

BER is the Building CO_2 Emission Rate expressed as $kgCO_2/(m^2.year)$.

Commissioning means the advancement of a fixed building service following installation, replacement or alteration of the whole or part of the system, from the state of static completion to working order by testing and adjusting as necessary to ensure that the system as a whole uses no more fuel and power than is reasonable in the circumstances, without prejudice to the need to comply with health and safety requirements. For each system *commissioning* includes setting-to-work, regulation (that is testing and adjusting repetitively) to achieve the specified performance, the calibration, setting up and testing of the associated automatic control systems, and recording of the system settings and the performance test results that have been accepted as satisfactory.

Controlled service or fitting means a service or fitting in relation to which Part G (sanitation, hot water safety and water efficiency), H (drainage and waste disposal), J (combustion appliances and fuel storage systems), L (conservation of fuel and power) or P (electrical safety) of Schedule 1 to the Building Regulations imposes a requirement.

Display window means an area of glazing, including glazed doors, intended for the display of products or services on offer within the building, positioned:

a. at the external perimeter of the building; and

b. at an access level and immediately adjacent to a pedestrian thoroughfare.

There should be no permanent workspace within one glazing height of the perimeter. Glazing more than 3 m above such an access level should not be considered part of a *display window* except:

a. where the products on display require a greater height of glazing;

b. in cases of building work involving changes to the façade and glazing requiring planning consent, where planners should have discretion to require a greater height of glazing, e.g. to fit in with surrounding buildings or to match the character of the existing façade.

It is expected that *display windows* will be found in Planning Use Classes A1, A2, A3 and D2 as detailed in Table 1.

Table 1 **Planning Use Classes**

Class	Use
A1	Shops: including retail-warehouse, undertakers, showrooms, post offices, hairdressers, shops for sale of cold food for consumption off premises
A2	Financial and professional services: banks, building societies, estate and employment agencies, betting offices
A3	Food and drink: restaurants, pubs, wine bars, shops for sale of hot food for consumption off premises
D2	Assembly and leisure: cinemas, concert halls, bingo halls, casinos, sports and leisure uses

Display lighting means lighting intended to highlight displays of exhibits or merchandise, or lighting used in spaces for public leisure and entertainment such as dance halls, auditoria, conference halls, restaurants and cinemas.

Dwelling means a self-contained unit designed to accommodate a single household. Buildings exclusively containing *rooms for residential purposes* such as nursing homes, student accommodation and similar are not *dwellings*, and in such cases, Approved Document L2A applies.

Emergency escape lighting means that part of emergency lighting that provides illumination for the safety of people leaving an area or attempting to terminate a dangerous process before leaving an area.

Energy efficiency requirements means the requirements of regulations 4A, 17C, 17D and 17E of, and Part L of Schedule 1 to, the Building Regulations.

*In respect of new buildings other than **dwellings**, the applicable requirements are those of Part L and regulation 17C.*

Fit-out work means that work needed to complete the partitioning and building services within the external fabric of the building (the shell) to meet the specific needs of incoming occupiers. **Fit-out work** can be carried out in whole or in parts:

a. in the same project and time frame as the construction of the building shell; or

b. at some time after the shell has been completed.

Fixed building services means any part of, or any controls associated with:

a. fixed internal or external lighting systems but does not include emergency escape lighting or specialist process lighting; or

b. fixed systems for heating, hot water service, air-conditioning or mechanical ventilation.

High usage entrance door means a door to an entrance primarily for the use of people that is expected to experience large traffic volumes, and where robustness and/or powered operation is the primary performance requirement. To qualify as a **high usage entrance door**, the door should be equipped with automatic closers and, except where operational requirements preclude, be protected by a lobby.

Room for residential purposes means a room, or a suite of rooms, which is not a dwelling-house or a flat and which is used by one or more persons to live and sleep and includes a room in a hostel, an hotel, a boarding house, a hall of residence or a residential home, whether or not the room is separated from or arranged in a cluster group with other rooms, but does not include a room in a hospital, or other similar establishment, used for patient accommodation and, for the purposes of this definition, a 'cluster' is a group of rooms for residential purposes which is:

a. separated from the rest of the building in which it is situated by a door which is designed to be locked; and

b. not designed to be occupied by a single household.

Specialist process lighting means lighting intended to illuminate specialist tasks within a space, rather than the space itself. It could include theatre spotlights, projection equipment, lighting in TV and photographic studios, medical lighting in operating theatres and doctors' and dentists' surgeries, illuminated signs, coloured or stroboscopic lighting, and art objects with integral lighting such as sculptures, decorative fountains and chandeliers.

TER is the Target CO_2 Emission Rate expressed as $kgCO_2/(m^2.year)$.

Total useful floor area is the total area of all enclosed spaces measured to the internal face of the external walls, that is to say it is the gross floor area as measured in accordance with the guidance issued to surveyors by the RICS. In this convention:

a. the area of sloping surfaces such as staircases, galleries, raked auditoria and tiered terraces should be taken as their area on plan; and

b. areas that are not enclosed such as open floors, covered ways and balconies are excluded.

Types of work covered by this Approved Document

3.2   This Approved Document is intended to give guidance on what, in ordinary circumstances, may be considered reasonable provision for compliance with the requirements of regulation 17C of, and Part L of Schedule 1 to, the Building Regulations in relation to works comprising:

a. The construction of new buildings other than **dwellings**.

b. **Fit-out works** where the work is either part of the construction of a new building, or is the first fit-out of a shell and core development where the shell is sold or let before the **fit-out work** is carried out. (Approved Document L2B applies to **fit-out works** in other circumstances.)

c. The construction of extensions to existing buildings that are not **dwellings** where the **total useful floor area** of the extension is greater than 100 m² and greater than 25 per cent of the **total useful floor area** of the existing building.

In addition this Approved Document gives guidance on compliance with regulations 20B, 20C and 20D of the Building Regulations and 12B, 12C and 12D of the Approved Inspectors Regulations.

3.3   When constructing a building that contains **dwellings**, account should also be taken of the guidance in Approved Document L1A. In most instances, Approved Document L1A should be used for guidance relating to the work on the individual **dwellings**, with this Approved Document L2A giving guidance relating to the parts of the building that are not a **dwelling**, such as heated common areas and, in the case of mixed-use developments, the commercial or retail space.

*It should be noted that **dwellings** refer to self-contained units. **Rooms for residential purposes** are not **dwellings**, and so for new buildings Approved Document L2A applies to, for instance, boarding houses, hostels and student accommodation blocks.*

3.4   If a building contains both living accommodation and space to be used for commercial purposes (e.g. workshop or office), the whole building should be treated as a **dwelling** as long as the commercial part could revert to domestic use. This could be the case if, for example:

a. there is direct access between the industrial or commercial space and the living accommodation; and

b. both are contained within the same thermal envelope; and

c. the living accommodation occupies a substantial proportion of the total area of the building.

*Sub-paragraph c means that a small manager's flat in a large non-domestic building would not mean the whole building should be treated as a **dwelling**. Similarly, the existence of a room used as an office or utility space within a **dwelling** would not mean that the building should not be treated as a **dwelling**.*

Buildings that are exempt from the energy efficiency requirements

3.5   New buildings other than **dwellings** which are roofed constructions having walls and which use energy to condition the indoor climate must comply with the **energy efficiency requirements** of the Building Regulations unless they are exempt. A building means the whole of a building or parts of it designed or altered to be used separately. The following classes of new buildings or parts of new buildings other than **dwellings** are exempt:

a. buildings which are used primarily or solely as places of worship;

b. temporary buildings with a planned time of use of 2 years or less, industrial sites, workshops and non-residential agricultural buildings with low energy demand;

c. stand-alone buildings other than **dwellings** with a **total useful floor area** of less than 50 m²;

d. some conservatories and porches.

3.6   The following paragraphs give guidance on those exemptions that relate to new buildings that are not **dwellings**.

a. **Places of worship:** For the purposes of the **energy efficiency requirements**, places of worship are taken to mean those buildings or parts of a building that are used for formal public worship, including adjoining spaces whose function is directly linked to that use (for example. a vestry in a church). Such parts of buildings of this type often have traditional, religious or cultural constraints that mean that compliance with the **energy efficiency requirements** would not be possible. Other parts of the building that are designed to be used separately, such as offices, catering facilities, day centres, meeting halls and accommodation, are not exempt.

b. **Temporary buildings:** For the purpose of the **energy efficiency requirements**, a temporary building with a planned time of use of two years or less does NOT include portable or modular buildings which have a planned service life greater than 2 years, whether on one or more sites.

c. **Industrial sites, workshops and non-residential agricultural buildings with low energy demand:** In relation to this category of exempt building, the low energy demand only relates to the energy used by fixed heating or cooling systems, NOT to energy required for or created by process needs. The following are examples of buildings in the above categories that are low energy demand:

i. buildings or parts of buildings where the space is not generally heated or cooled other than by process heat;

ii. buildings or parts of buildings that only require heating or cooling for short periods each year, such as during critical periods in the production cycle (e.g. plant germination, egg hatching) or in very severe weather conditions.

Industrial sites, workshops and non-residential agricultural buildings are exempt only if they meet the low energy demand criterion. In other cases, such buildings must comply with **energy efficiency requirements**. Similarly, other buildings (e.g. some types of warehouse) may have low energy demand but are not exempt because they do not fall into one of the above categories.

Special considerations

3.7   Special considerations apply to certain classes of non-exempt building. These building types are:

a. non-exempt buildings with low energy demand; the guidance specific to such buildings is given in paragraphs 3.8 to 3.11;

b. modular and portable buildings with a planned time of use of more than two years (at one or more sites); the guidance specific to such buildings is given in the section beginning with paragraph 4.20;

c. shell and core developments; the guidance specific to such buildings is given in the section beginning with paragraph 4.25.

Non-exempt buildings with low energy demand

3.8   For the purposes of this Approved Document, non-exempt buildings with low energy demand are taken to be those buildings or parts thereof where:

a. **fixed building services** for heating and/or cooling are either not provided, or are provided only to heat or cool a localised area rather than the entire enclosed volume of the space concerned (e.g. localised radiant heaters at a workstation in a generally unheated space); or

b. **fixed building services** are used to heat space in the building to temperatures substantially less than those normally provided for human comfort (e.g. to provide condensation or frost protection in a warehouse).

3.9 In such situations, it is not reasonable to expect the entire building envelope to be insulated to the standard expected for more typical buildings. In such situations, no **TER/BER** calculation is required, but reasonable provision would be for every **fixed building service** that is installed to meet the energy efficiency standards set out in the *Non-Domestic Building Services Compliance Guide*[1]. In addition, the building envelope should be insulated to a degree that is reasonable in the particular case. If some general heating is provided (case (b) above), then it would be reasonable that no part of the opaque fabric had a U-value worse than 0.7 W/m²·K.

3.10 If a part of a building with low energy demand is partitioned off and heated normally (e.g. an office area in an unheated warehouse), the separately heated area should be treated as a separate 'building' and the normal procedures for demonstrating compliance (including a **TER/BER** calculation) should be followed in respect of the enclosure.

3.11 If a building with low energy demand subsequently changes such that the space is generally conditioned, then this is likely to involve the initial provision or an increase in the installed capacity of a **fixed building service**. Such activities are covered by Regulation 17D. The guidance in ADL2B would require the building envelope to be upgraded and a consequential improvement to be made, a process that is likely to be much more expensive than incorporating suitable levels of insulation at the new-build stage. Alternatively, if the building shell was designed as a building with low energy demand and the first occupier of the building wanted to install (e.g.) heating, this would be first **fit-out works**, and a full **TER/BER** submission would then be required (see paragraph 3.2b).

Notification of work covered by the energy efficiency requirements

3.12 In almost all cases of constructing new buildings other than **dwellings** it will be necessary to notify a **BCB** in advance of any work starting except as set out in paragraphs 3.13 to 3.17 below.

Competent person self-certification schemes

3.13 It is not necessary to notify a **BCB** in advance of work which is to be carried out by a person registered with a relevant competent person self-certification scheme listed in Schedule 2A to the Building Regulations. In order to join such a scheme a person must demonstrate competence to carry out the type of work the scheme covers, and also the ability to comply with all relevant requirements in the Building Regulations.

3.14 Where work is carried out by a person registered with a competent person scheme, regulation 16A of the Building Regulations 2000 and regulation 11A of the Building (Approved Inspectors etc) Regulations 2000 require that the occupier of the building be given, within 30 days of the completion of the work, a certificate confirming that the work complies fully with all applicable building regulation requirements. There is also a requirement to give the **BCB** a notice of the work carried out, again within 30 days of the completion of the work. These certificates and notices are usually made available thorough the scheme operator.

3.15 **BCBs** are authorised to accept these certificates and notices as evidence of compliance with the requirements of the Building Regulations. Local authority inspection and enforcement powers remain unaffected, although they are normally used only in response to a complaint that work does not comply.

3.16 There are no competent person schemes which cover all aspects of the construction of a new building other than a **dwelling**. There are, however, schemes which cover the installation of **fixed building services** (heating, hot water, air-conditioning and mechanical ventilation).

3.17 A list of competent person self-certification schemes with the types of work for which they are authorised can be found at www.communities.gov.uk.

Materials and workmanship

3.18 Any building work which is subject to the requirements imposed by Schedule 1 to the Building Regulations should, in accordance with regulation 7, be carried out with proper materials and in a workmanlike manner.

3.19 You may show that you have complied with regulation 7 in a number of ways. These include demonstrating the appropriate use of:

- a product bearing CE marking in accordance with the Construction Products Directive (89/106/EC)[2] as amended by the CE Marking Directive (93/68/EC)[3], the Low Voltage Directive (2006/95/EC)[4] and the EMC Directive (2004/108/ EC)[5];

- a product complying with an appropriate technical specification (as defined in those Directives mentioned above), a British Standard, or an alternative national technical specification of a Member State of the European Union or Turkey[6], or of another State signatory to the Agreement on the European Economic Area (EEA) that provides an equivalent level of safety and protection;

---

[1] Non-domestic Building Services Compliance Guide, CLG, 2010

[2] As implemented by the Construction Products Regulations 1991 (SI 1991/1620).

[3] As implemented by the Construction Products (Amendment) Regulations 1994 (SI 1994/3051).

[4] As implemented by the Electrical Equipment (Safety) Regulations 1994 (SI 1994/3260).

[5] As implemented by the Electromagnetic Compatibility Regulations 2006 (SI 2006/3418).

[6] Decision No 1/95 of the EC-Turkey Association Council of 22 December 1995.

- a product covered by a national or European certificate issued by a European Technical Approval Issuing body, provided the conditions of use are in accordance with the terms of the certificate.

3.20 You will find further guidance in the Approved Document which specifically supports regulation 7 on materials and workmanship.

Independent certification schemes

3.21 There are many UK product certification schemes. Such schemes certify compliance with the requirements of a recognised document that is appropriate to the purpose for which the material is to be used. Materials which are not so certified may still conform to a relevant standard.

3.22 Many certification bodies that approve such schemes are accredited by the United Kingdom Accreditation Service (UKAS). Such bodies can issue certificates only for the categories of product covered under the terms of their accreditation.

3.23 **BCBs** may take into account the certification of products, components, materials or structures under such schemes as evidence of compliance with the relevant standard. Similarly, **BCBs** may accept the certification of the installation or maintenance of products, components, materials or structures under such schemes as evidence of compliance with the relevant standard. Nonetheless, before accepting that certification constitutes compliance with building regulations, a **BCB** should establish in advance that the relevant scheme is adequate for that purpose.

Standards and technical specifications

3.24 Building regulations are made for specific purposes, including securing the health, safety, welfare and convenience of people in or about buildings; furthering the conservation of fuel and power; furthering the protection or enhancement of the environment; and facilitating sustainable development. Guidance contained in standards and technical approvals is relevant to the extent that it relates to those purposes. However, it should be noted that guidance may also address other aspects of performance such as serviceability, or aspects which, although they relate to health and safety, are not covered by building regulations.

3.25 When an Approved Document makes reference to a named standard or document, the relevant version of the standard or document is the one listed at the end of the Approved Document. If this version has been revised or updated by the issuing standards body, the latest version may be used as a source of guidance provided it continues to address the relevant requirements of the Building Regulations. However, until the reference in the Approved Document is revised, the standard or document listed remains the approved source.

3.26 The appropriate use of a product that complies with a European Technical Approval as defined in the Construction Products Directive will meet the relevant requirements.

3.27 Communities and Local Government intends to issue periodic amendments to its Approved Documents to reflect emerging harmonised European Standards. Where a national standard is to be replaced by a European harmonised standard, there will be a coexistence period during which either standard may be referred to. At the end of the coexistence period the national standard will be withdrawn.

The Workplace (Health, Safety and Welfare) Regulations 1992

3.28 The Workplace (Health, Safety and Welfare) Regulations 1992, as amended, apply to the common parts of flats and similar buildings if people such as cleaners, wardens and caretakers are employed to work in these common parts. These Regulations contain some requirements which affect building design. The main requirements are now covered by the Building Regulations, but for further information see *Workplace health, safety and welfare, Workplace (Health, Safety and Welfare) Regulations 1992, Approved Code of Practice and guidance*, HSE publication L24, HMSO,1996.

3.29 Where the requirements of the Building Regulations that are covered by this Approved Document do not apply to *dwellings*, the provisions may still be required in the situations described above in order to satisfy the Workplace Regulations.

Demonstrating compliance

3.30 In the Secretary of State's view, compliance with the *energy efficiency requirements* could be demonstrated by meeting the five separate criteria set out in the following paragraphs. It is expected that compliance software will produce an output report that will assist **BCBs** check that compliance has been achieved.

*The output report can benefit both developers and **BCBs** during the design and construction stages as well as at completion.*

3.31 Criterion 1: in accordance with regulation 17C, the calculated CO_2 emission rate for the building (the Building Emission Rate, **BER**) must not be greater than the Target CO_2 Emission Rate (**TER**), which is determined by following the procedures set out in paragraphs 4.7 to 4.27.

Criterion 1 is a regulation and is therefore mandatory, whereas Criteria 2 to 5 are only guidance. The calculations required as part of the procedure used to show compliance with this criterion can also provide information needed to prepare the Energy Performance Certificate required by regulation 17E of the Building Regulations and by the Energy Performance of Buildings (Certificates and Inspections) (England and Wales) Regulations 2007 (SI 2007/991) as amended.

3.32   Criterion 2: the performance of the building fabric and the heating, hot water and fixed lighting systems should achieve reasonable overall standards of energy efficiency following the procedure set out in paragraphs 4.28 to 4.40.

This is intended to place limits on design flexibility to discourage excessive and inappropriate trade-offs – e.g. buildings with poor insulation standards offset by renewable energy systems with uncertain service lives. This emphasises the purpose of Criterion 2.

3.33   Criterion 3: demonstrate that the building has appropriate passive control measures to limit solar gains. The guidance given in paragraphs 4.41 to 4.44 of this Approved Document provides a way of demonstrating that suitable provisions have been made.

The purpose is to limit solar gains to reasonable levels during the summer period, in order to reduce the need for or installed capacity of air-conditioning systems.

3.34   Criterion 4: the performance of the building, as built, should be consistent with the **BER**. The guidance in Section 5 can be used to show that this criterion has been met. Extra credits will be given in the **TER/BER** calculation where builders provide robust evidence of quality-assured procedures in the design and construction phases; and

3.35   Criterion 5: the necessary provisions for enabling energy-efficient operation of the building should be put in place. The procedures described in Section 6 can be used to show that this criterion has been met.

Special areas

3.36   The following paragraphs describe some 'special areas' that fall outside the normal five criteria, and give guidance on how reasonable provision for the conservation of fuel and power can be demonstrated.

Conservatories and porches

3.37   Where conservatories and porches are installed at the same time as the construction of a new building follow the guidance in Approved Document L2B.

Swimming pool basins

3.38   Where a swimming pool is constructed as part of a new building, reasonable provision should be made to limit heat loss from the pool basin by achieving a U-value no worse than 0.25 W/m².K as calculated according to BS EN ISO 13370[7].

3.39   In terms of Criterion 1, the building should be assessed as if the pool basin were not there, although the pool hall should be included. The area covered by the pool should be replaced with the equivalent area of floor with the same U-value as the pool surround.

---

[7]   BS EN ISO 13370 *Thermal performance of buildings. Heat transfer via the ground. Calculation methods.*

Section 4: Design standards

REGULATIONS 17A AND 17B

4.1   Regulations 17A, 17B and 17C of the Building Regulations implement Articles 3, 4 and 5 of the Energy Performance of Buildings Directive. Regulations 17A and 17B state that:

Methodology of calculation of the energy performance of buildings

17A.–(1) The Secretary of State shall approve–

a. a methodology of calculation of the energy performance of buildings, including methods for calculating asset ratings and operational ratings of buildings; and

b. ways in which the energy performance of buildings, as calculated in accordance with the methodology, shall be expressed.

(2) In this regulation–

'asset rating' means a numerical indicator of the amount of energy estimated to meet the different needs associated with a standardised use of the building; and

'operational rating' means a numerical indicator of the amount of energy consumed during the occupation of the building over a period of time.

Minimum energy performance requirements for buildings

17B.–The Secretary of State shall approve minimum energy performance requirements for new buildings, in the form of target CO_2 emission rates, which shall be based upon the methodology approved pursuant to regulation 17A.

Target carbon dioxide Emission Rate (TER)

4.2   The Target CO_2 Emission Rate (**TER**) is the minimum energy performance requirement for a new building based on the methodology approved by the Secretary of State in accordance with regulation 17B. It is expressed in terms of the mass of CO_2 emitted per year per square metre of the **total useful floor area** of the building ($kg/m^2/year$).

4.3   The **TER** must be calculated using one of the calculation tools included in the methodology approved by the Secretary of State for calculating the energy performance of buildings pursuant to regulation 17A. Those tools include:

a. the Simplified Building Energy Model (SBEM)[8] for those buildings whose design features are capable of being adequately modelled by SBEM; or

b. other software tools approved under the Notice of Approval[9].

4.4   From time to time further software may be approved. An up-to-date list can be found on the Department's website at www.communities.gov.uk

4.5   As part of the submission to a **BCB**, the applicant must show that the software tool used is appropriate to the application.

4.6   The **TER** is established by using approved software to calculate the CO_2 emission rate from a notional building of the same size and shape as the actual building, but with specified properties. These specified properties shall be as set out in the 2010 NCM Modelling Guide[10], in the section headed 'Detailed definition of Notional Building for buildings other than dwellings'. The key components of the notional building specification can also be seen at Table 6 in the Impact Assessment[11]. The **TER** is set equal to the CO_2 emissions from this notional building, with no further adjustment being made.

*Note that the **TER** is no longer based on a 2002 notional building and an improvement factor; for 2010 it is based on a building of the same size and shape as the actual building, constructed to a concurrent specification. This concurrent specification for Part L 2010 is given in the 2010 NCM modelling guide. Developers are still given the freedom to vary the specification, provided the same overall level of CO_2 emissions is achieved or bettered. This approach to target setting has been adopted because the level of improvement that can be reasonably expected varies significantly by building sector, and so a blanket improvement factor would be inequitable. The specification delivers an overall 25 per cent reduction in CO_2 emissions across the new-build mix for the non-dwellings sector (the so-called 'aggregate approach'). Some building types will be required to improve by more than 25 per cent, some by less, but all should achieve the required level of improvement at approximately the same cost of carbon mitigation.*

CRITERION 1 – ACHIEVING THE BER

4.7   Regulation 17C states that:

New buildings

17C. Where a building is erected, it shall not exceed the target CO_2 emission rate for the building that has been approved pursuant to regulation 17B.

---

8   Simplified Building Energy Model (SBEM) User manual and software, available at www.2010ncm.bre.co.uk

9   Notice of Approval of the methodology of calculation of the energy performance of buildings in England and Wales

10   National Calculation Methodology (NCM) modelling guide (for buildings other than dwellings in England and Wales), CLG, 2010

11   Implementation Stage Impact Assessment of Revisions to Parts F and L of the Building Regulations from 2010, CLG, March 2010

Calculating the CO_2 emissions from the actual building

4.8   To demonstrate that the requirement in regulation 17C has been met, the actual Building CO_2 Emission Rate (**BER**) must be no greater (no worse) than the **TER** calculated as set out in paragraphs 4.2 to 4.6.

4.9   The **BER** must be calculated using the same calculation tool as used for establishing the **TER**.

CO_2 emission rate calculations

4.10   Regulation 20D[12] of the Building Regulations states:

20D.–(1) This regulation applies where a building is erected and regulation 17C applies.

(2) Not later than the day before the work starts, the person carrying out the work shall give the local authority a notice which specifies–

a.   the target CO_2 emission rate for the building,

b.   the calculated CO_2 emission rate for the building as designed, and

c.   a list of specifications to which the building is to be constructed.

(3) Not later than five days after the work has been completed, the person carrying out the work shall give the local authority–

a.   a notice which specifies–

   i.   the target CO_2 emission rate for the building,

   ii.   the calculated CO_2 emission rate for the building as constructed, and

   iii.   whether the building has been constructed in accordance with the list of specifications referred to in paragraph (2)(c), and if not a list of any changes to those specifications; or

b.   a certificate of the sort referred to in paragraph (4) accompanied by the information referred to in sub-paragraph (a).

(4) A local authority is authorised to accept, as evidence that the requirements of regulation 17C have been satisfied, a certificate to that effect by an energy assessor who is accredited to produce such certificates for that category of building.

(5) In this regulation –

'energy assessor' means an individual who is a member of an accreditation scheme approved by the Secretary of State in accordance with regulation 17F; and

'specifications' means specifications used for the calculation of the CO_2 emission rate.

CO_2 emission rate calculation *before commencement of work*

4.11   As required by regulations 17C and 20D, before the work starts, the builder shall carry out a calculation that demonstrates that the **BER** of the building as designed is not greater than the **TER**. This design-based calculation shall be provided to the **BCB**, along with a list of specifications of the building envelope and the *fixed building services* used in calculating the **BER**.

This design stage calculation and provision of a list of specifications will assist the BCB to confirm that what is being built aligns with the claimed performance. As set out at Appendix A it is expected that compliance software will be used to produce the list of specifications and highlight those features of the design that are critical to achieving compliance. These 'key features' can be used to prioritise the risk-based inspection of the building as part of confirming compliance with Regulation 17C. If a provisional energy rating is calculated at this stage and an interim recommendations report is therefore available, the recommendations should be reviewed by the developer to see if further carbon mitigation measures might be incorporated in a cost-effective manner.

CO_2 emission rate calculation *after completion*

4.12   After work has been completed, the builder must notify the **BCB** of the **TER** and **BER** and whether the building has been constructed in accordance with the list of specifications submitted to the **BCB** before work started. If not, a list of any changes to the design-stage list of specifications must be given to the **BCB**. **BCB**s are authorised to accept, as evidence of compliance, a certificate to this effect signed off by a suitably accredited energy assessor.

It would be useful to provide additional information to support the values used in the BER calculation and the list of specifications. For example, U-values might be determined from a specific calculation, in which case the details should be provided, or from an accredited source, in which case a reference to that source would be sufficient. It would also be useful if evidence was provided that demonstrates that the building as designed satisfies the requirements of Criteria 2 and 3.

4.13   In order to determine the **BER**, the CO_2 emission factors shall be as specified in the paper published by DECC[13].

4.14   When systems are capable of being fired by more than one fuel, then:

---

[12]   There is a similar regulation (regulation 12D) in the Building (Approved Inspectors etc.) Regulations 2000 (SI 2000/2532) which applies when an approved inspector is the BCB.

[13]   See Table 12 at www.bre.co.uk/sap2009

a. Where a biomass heating appliance is supplemented by an alternative appliance (e.g. gas), the CO_2 emission factor for the overall heating system should be based on a weighted average for the two fuels based on the anticipated usage of those fuels. The **BER** submission should be accompanied by a report, signed by a suitably qualified person, detailing how the combined emission factor has been derived.

b. Where the same appliance is capable of burning both biomass fuel and fossil fuel, the CO_2 emission factor for dual fuel appliances should be used, except where the building is in a smoke control area, when the anthracite figure should be used.

c. In all other cases, the fuel with the highest CO_2 emission factor should be used.

This option is to cover dual fuel systems, where the choice of fuel actually used depends on prevailing market prices.

4.15 If thermal energy is supplied from a district or community heating or cooling system, emission factors should be determined by considering the particular details of the scheme. Calculations should take account of the annual average performance of the whole system (i.e. the distribution circuits and all the heat generating plant, including any Combined Heat and Power (CHP), and any waste heat recovery or heat dumping). The electricity generated by any CHP or trigeneration scheme is always credited at an emission factor equal to the grid average. CO_2 emissions associated with the thermal energy streams of a trigeneration scheme should be attributed in proportion to the output energy streams. The **BER** submission should be accompanied by a report, signed by a suitably qualified person, detailing how the emission factors have been derived.

This means that if a trigeneration scheme burns F kWh of input fuel to produce E kWh of electricity, H kWh of useful heat and C kWh of useful cooling, the emission factor for the heat and coolth output should both be taken as $1/(H+C)*(F*CO2_F - E*CO2_E)$ where CO_{2F} is the emission factor for the input fuel, and CO_{2E} the factor for grid electricity.

See NCM Modelling Guide at www.communities.gov.uk.

Achieving the TER

4.16 Certain management features offer improved energy efficiency in practice. Where these management features are provided in the actual building, the **BER** can be reduced by an amount equal to the product of the factor given in Table 2 and the CO_2 emissions for the system(s) to which the feature is applied.

*For example, if the CO_2 emissions due to electrical energy consumption were 70 kgCO$_2$/(m^2.year) without power factor correction, the provision of correction equipment to achieve a power factor of 0.95 would enable the **BER** to be reduced by 70 x 0.025 = 1.75 kgCO$_2$/(m^2.year).*

4.17 Provided the building satisfies the limits on design flexibility as set out in Criterion 2, the compliance procedure allows the designer full flexibility to achieve the **TER** utilising fabric and system measures and the integration of low and zero carbon (LZC) technologies in whatever mix is appropriate to the scheme. The approved compliance tools include appropriate algorithms that enable the designer to assess the role LZC technologies (including local renewable and low-carbon schemes driven by planning requirements[14]) can play in achieving the **TER**.

Table 2 **Enhanced management and control features**

Feature	Adjustment factor
Automatic monitoring and targeting with alarms for out of range values[1]	0.050
Power factor correction to achieve a whole building power factor > 0.90[2]	0.010
Power factor correction to achieve a whole building power factor > 0.95[2]	0.025

Notes:

1 Automatic monitoring and targeting with alarms for out of range values means a complete installation that measures, records, transmits, analyses, reports and communicates meaningful energy management information to enable the operator to manage the energy it uses.

2 The power factor adjustment can be taken only if the whole building power factor is corrected to the level stated. The two levels of power factor correction are alternative values, not additive.

[14] See the Planning Policy Statement: *Planning and Climate Change* and its supporting practice guidance at www.communities.gov.uk/planningandbuilding/planning/planningpolicyguidance/planningpolicystatements/planningpolicystatements/ppsclimatechange/

4.18   In order to facilitate incorporation of improvements in system efficiencies and the integration with LZC technologies, the designer should:

a.   consider adopting heating and cooling systems that use low distribution temperatures; and

b.   where multiple systems serve the same end use, organise the control strategies such that priority is given to the least carbon-intensive option; and

For example, where a solar hot water system is available, the controls should be arranged so that the best use is made of the available solar energy.

c.   consider making the building easily adaptable by facilitating the integration of additional LZC technologies at a later date. Providing appropriate facilities at the construction stage can make subsequent enhancements much easier and cheaper, e.g. providing capped off connections that can link into a planned community heating scheme.

4.19   Similarly, the designer should consider the potential impact of future climate change on the performance of the building. This might include giving consideration to how a cooling system might be provided at some future point.

Special considerations: Modular and portable buildings with a planned time of use of more than two years

4.20   Special considerations apply to modular and portable buildings (see paragraph 3.7). The following paragraphs detail what is considered as reasonable provision for a variety of different circumstances.

The placing of an existing module to a new site is considered to be the construction of a new building as far as the Building Regulations are concerned. In that context, it is not always appropriate to expect such a relocated unit to meet the new-build standards set out in this Approved Document, especially as the embodied energy in an existing module is retained, a benefit that compensates for small differences in operating energy demand. Further, portable buildings are often 'distress purchases', and the constraints imposed by the time in which a working building must be delivered mean that additional considerations apply.

At given location

4.21   Compliance with the *energy efficiency requirements* should be demonstrated by showing that satisfactory performance has been achieved against each of the five compliance criteria set out in this Approved Document. However, if more than 70 per cent of the external envelope of the building is to be created from sub-assemblies manufactured prior to the date this Approved Document comes into force, the *TER* should be adjusted by the relevant factor from Table 3. One way of demonstrating the date of manufacture of each sub-assembly is by relating the serial number to the manufacturer's records. If the units are to be refurbished as part of the process, then the guidance in Approved Document L2B should be followed in terms of the standards to be achieved, e.g. for replacement windows and new lighting.

At more than one location

4.22   Portable buildings with an intended planned time of use in a given location of less than 2 years are often 'distress purchases' (e.g. following a fire), and the buildings must be up and operational in a matter of days. In such cases, different arrangements for demonstrating compliance with regulation 17C apply, as set out in the following paragraphs. An example of the evidence that the planned time of use in the given location is less than 2 years would be the hire agreement for the unit.

4.23   In the case of a modular or portable building intended to be sited in a given location for less than 2 years, a *TER/BER* calculation should be carried out when the module is first constructed and can be based on a standard generic configuration. This calculation can then be provided as evidence of satisfying the requirements of Regulation 17C whenever the building is moved to a new location, always provided its intended time of use in that new location is less than 2 years. In addition to the details of the calculation, the supplier should provide written confirmation that:

a.   the modules as actually provided meet or exceed the elemental energy standards of the generic module on which the calculation was based; and

b.   the activities assumed in the generic module are reasonably representative of the planned use of the actual module.

4.24   It is recognised that in situations where the planned time of use in a given location is less than 2 years, the only practical heating technology is electric resistance heating. In such cases, reasonable provision would be to provide energy efficiency measures that are 15 per cent better than if using conventional fossil fuel heating. This can be demonstrated by assuming that the heating in the generic configuration used for the *TER/BER* calculation is provided by a gas boiler with an efficiency of 77 per cent. Post initial construction, any work on the module should meet the standards set out in ADL2B. If a *TER/BER* calculation is not available for a module constructed prior to 1 October 2010, reasonable provision would be to demonstrate that the BER is not greater than the 2010 *TER* adjusted by the relevant factor from Table 3.

Table 3 TER multiplying factor for modular and portable buildings

Date of manufacture of 70% of modules making up the external envelope	TER multiplying factor
After 1 Oct 2010	1.00
6 April 2006 – 1 Oct 2010	1.33
1 April 2002 – 5 April 2006	1.75
Pre 1 April 2002	1.75 [2.35[1]]

Notes:

1 For buildings with a planned time of use in a given location of less than 2 years, the figure in brackets is applicable.

Shell and core developments

4.25 If a building is offered to the market for sale or let as a shell for specific *fit-out work* by the incoming occupier, the developer should demonstrate via the design-stage *TER/BER* submission how the building shell as offered could meet the *energy efficiency requirements*. For those parts of the building where certain systems are not installed at the point the building is to be offered to the market, the model that is used to derive the *BER* will have to assume efficiencies for those services that will be installed as part of the first *fit-out work*. The specification provided to the *BCB* (see paragraph 4.11) should identify which services have not been provided in the base build, and the efficiency values assumed for each such system. This will enable the *BCB* to ensure that the necessary infrastructure needed to deliver the assumed fit-out specification is provided as part of the base build. At practical completion of the base building, the as-built *TER/BER* calculation should be based only on the building and systems as actually constructed; the fit-out areas should be assumed to be conditioned to temperatures appropriate to their designated use, but no associated energy demand included.

As part of the design-stage calculation, a predicted EPC rating for the fit-out areas should be available to inform prospective occupiers of the energy performance that is achievable. However, a formal EPC lodged on the EPC register is not required at this stage.

4.26 When an incoming occupier does first *fit-out work* on all or part of the building through the provision or extension of any of the fixed services for heating, hot water, air-conditioning or mechanical ventilation, then *TER/BER* submission should be made to the *BCB* after completion to demonstrate compliance for the part of the building covered by the *fit-out* work. This submission should be based on the building shell as constructed and the *fixed building services* as actually installed. If the *fit-out work* does not include the provision or extension of any of the fixed services for heating, hot water, air-conditioning or mechanical ventilation, then

reasonable provision would be to demonstrate that any lighting systems that are installed are at least as efficient as those assumed in the shell developer's initial submission.

Since the fit-out is specific to the needs of the particular tenant and is, by definition, uniquely controlled by him for his benefit, this is creating a new 'part designed or altered for separate use', and under regulation 17E a new EPC is required for that part of the physical building covered by the fit-out.

Industrial sites, workshops and non-residential agricultural buildings other than those with low energy demand

4.27 Special considerations may apply in such cases, e.g. where a CO_2 target is established through other regulatory frameworks such as the carbon reduction commitment, or where it is impractical for the generic National Calculation Methodology to adequately account for the particular industrial processes or agricultural use without leading to the possibility of negative impacts on cost-effectiveness and/or increased technical risk. In such cases, reasonable provision would be to provide *fixed building services* that satisfy the standards set out in Approved Document L2B.

CRITERION 2 – LIMITS ON DESIGN FLEXIBILITY

4.28 While the approach to complying with Criterion 1 allows considerable design flexibility, paragraph L1(a)(i) of Schedule 1 to the Building Regulations requires that reasonable provision should be made to limit heat gains and losses through the fabric of the building, and paragraphs L1(b)(i) and (ii) require that energy-efficient *fixed building services* and effective controls be provided.

4.29 One way of showing that the requirement has been satisfied is to demonstrate that the fabric elements and the *fixed building services* all satisfy minimum energy efficiency standards as specified in the following paragraphs.

Note that in order to satisfy the TER, the building specification will need to be considerably better than the stated values in many aspects of the design.

Fabric standards

4.30 Table 4 sets out the worst acceptable standards for fabric properties. The stated value represents the area-weighted average value for all elements of that type. In general, achievement of the *TER* is likely to require better fabric performance than set out in Table 4.

4.31   U-values shall be calculated using the methods and conventions set out in BR 443[15], and should be based on the whole unit (i.e. in the case of a window, the combined performance of the glazing and the frame). The U-value of glazing can be calculated for:

a.   the smaller of the two standard windows defined in BS EN 14351-1[16]; or

b.   the standard window configuration set out in BR 443; or

c.   the specific size and configuration of the actual window.

For domestic-type construction, SAP 2009 Table 6e gives values for different window configurations that can be used in the absence of test data or calculated values.

4.32   The U-values for roof windows and rooflights given in this Approved Document are based on the U-value having been assessed with the roof window or rooflight in the vertical position. If a particular unit has been assessed in a plane other than the vertical, the standards given in this Approved Document should be modified by making an adjustment that is dependent on the slope of the unit following the guidance given in BR 443.

Table 4 **Limiting fabric parameters**

Roof	0.25 W/m².K
Wall	0.35 W/m².K
Floor	0.25 W/m².K
Windows, roof windows, rooflights[3], curtain walling and pedestrian doors[1,2]	2.2 W/m².K
Vehicle access and similar large doors	1.5 W/m².K
High-usage entrance doors	3.5 W/m².K
Roof ventilators (inc. smoke vents)	3.5 W/m².K
Air permeability	10.0 m³/h.m² at 50 Pa

Notes:

1   Excluding display windows and similar glazing. There is no limit on design flexibility for these exclusions but their impact on CO_2 emissions must be taken into account in calculations.

2   In buildings with high internal heat gains, a less demanding area weighted average U-value for the glazing may be an appropriate way of reducing overall CO_2 emissions and hence the BER. If this case can be made, then the average U-value for windows can be relaxed from the values given above. However, values should be no worse than 2.7 W/m².K.

3   The relevant rooflight U-value for checking against these limits is that based on the developed area of the rooflight, not the area of the roof aperture.

Approved Document C gives limiting values for individual elements to minimise condensation risk.

[15]   BR 443 *Conventions for U-value calculations*, BRE, 2006.
[16]   EN 14351-1, *Windows and doors – Product standard, performance characteristics*, 2006.

Design limits for building services

4.33   This section sets out the design limits for *fixed building services* to meet the requirements of Part L1(b).

Controls

4.34   Systems should be provided with appropriate controls to enable the achievement of reasonable standards of energy efficiency in use. In normal circumstances, the following features would be appropriate for heating, ventilation and air-conditioning system controls:

a.   The systems should be subdivided into separate control zones to correspond to each area of the building that has a significantly different solar exposure, or pattern or type of use; and

b.   Each separate control zone should be capable of independent timing and temperature control and, where appropriate, ventilation and air recirculation rate; and

c.   The provision of the service should respond to the requirements of the space it serves. If both heating and cooling are provided, they should be controlled so as not to operate simultaneously; and

d.   Central plant should operate only as and when the zone systems require it. The default condition should be off.

4.35   In addition to these general control provisions, the systems should meet specific control and efficiency standards as set out in the paragraphs below.

System efficiencies

4.36   Each *fixed building service* should be at least as efficient as the worst acceptable value for the particular type of appliance as set out in the *Non-Domestic Building Services Compliance Guide*. If the type of appliance is not covered by the Guide, then reasonable provision would be to demonstrate that the proposed system is not less efficient than a comparable system that is covered by the Guide.

To not inhibit innovation.

4.37   The efficiency claimed for the *fixed building service* should be based on the appropriate test standard as set out in the *Non-Domestic Building Services Compliance Guide* and the test data should be certified by a notified body. It would be reasonable for *BCBs* to accept such data at face value. In the absence of such quality-assured data, the *BCB* should satisfy itself that the claimed performance is justified.

Energy meters

4.38   Reasonable provision for energy meters would be install energy metering systems that enable:

a.   at least 90 per cent of the estimated annual energy consumption of each fuel to be assigned to the various end-use categories (heating, lighting etc.). Detailed guidance on how this can be achieved is given in CIBSE TM 39[17]; and

b. the output of any renewable energy system to be separately monitored; and

c. in buildings with a **total useful floor area** greater than 1000m^2, automatic meter reading and data collection facilities.

4.39 The metering provisions should be designed such as to facilitate the benchmarking of energy performance as set out in TM 46[18].

Centralised switching of appliances

4.40 Consideration should be given to the provision of centralised switches to allow the facilities manager to switch off appliances when they are not needed (e.g. overnight and at weekends). Where appropriate, these should be automated (with manual override) so that energy savings are maximised.

A centralised switch would be more reliable than depending on each individual occupant to switch off their (e.g.) computer.

CRITERION 3 – LIMITING THE EFFECTS OF SOLAR GAINS IN SUMMER

4.41 This section sets out the approach to limiting heat gains as required by paragraph L1(a)(i) of Schedule 1 to the Building Regulations.

4.42 The following guidance applies to all buildings, irrespective of whether they are air conditioned or not. The intention is to limit solar gains during the summer period to either:

a. reduce the need for air-conditioning; or

b. reduce the installed capacity of any air-conditioning system that is installed.

4.43 If the criterion set out below is satisfied in the context of a naturally ventilated building, this is NOT evidence that the internal environment of the building will be satisfactory, since many factors that are not covered by the compliance assessment procedure will have a bearing on the incidence of overheating (incidental gains, thermal capacity, ventilation provisions, etc.).

Therefore the developer should work with the design team to specify what constitutes an acceptable indoor environment in the particular case, and carry out the necessary design assessments to develop solutions that meet the agreed brief. Some ways of assessing overheating risk are given in CIBSE TM37[19] and, for education buildings, in BB101[20].

4.44 For the purposes of Part L, reasonable provision for limiting solar gain through the building fabric would be demonstrated by showing that, for each space in the building that is either occupied or mechanically cooled, the solar gains through the glazing aggregated over the period from April to September inclusive are no greater than would occur through one of the following reference glazing systems with a defined total solar energy transmittance (g-value) calculated according to BS EN 410[21]:

a. For every space that is defined in the NCM database as being side lit, the reference case is an east-facing façade with full-width glazing to a height of 1.0m having a framing factor of 10 per cent and a normal solar energy transmittance (g-value) of 0.68.

b. For every space that is defined in the NCM database as being top lit, and whose average zone height is not greater than 6m, the reference case is a horizontal roof of the same total area that is 10 per cent glazed as viewed from the inside out and having rooflights that have a framing factor of 25 per cent and a normal solar energy transmittance (g-value) of 0.68.

c. For every space that is defined in the NCM database as being top lit and whose average zone height is greater than 6m, the reference case is a horizontal roof of the same total area that is 20 per cent glazed as viewed from the inside out and having rooflights that have a framing factor of 15 per cent and a normal solar energy transmittance (g-value) of 0.46;

In double-height industrial-type spaces, dirt on the rooflights and internal absorption within the rooflight reduce solar gains. These effects, combined with temperature stratification, will reduce the impact of solar gains in the occupied space and so increased rooflight area may be justified. In such situations, the developer should pay particular attention to the design assessments referred to in paragraph 4.44b.

d. For the purpose of this specific guidance, an occupied space means a space that is intended to be occupied by the same person for a substantial part of the day. This excludes circulation spaces, and other areas of transient occupancy, such as toilets, as well as spaces that are not intended for occupation (e.g. **display windows**).

---

[17]   TM 39 *Building energy metering*, CIBSE, 2010.
[18]   TM 46 *Energy benchmarks*, CIBSE, 2008.
[19]   TM37 *Design for improved solar shading control*, CIBSE, 2006.
[20]   *Ventilation of school buildings*, Building bulletin 101, School Building and Design Unit, Department for Education and Skills, 2006. See www.teachernet.gov.uk/iaq

---

[21]   BS EN 410 *Glass in building: Determination of luminous and solar characteristics of glazing*, BSI, 1998.

Section 5: Quality of construction and commissioning

CRITERION 4 – BUILDING PERFORMANCE CONSISTENT WITH BER

5.1 Buildings should be constructed and equipped so that performance is consistent with the calculated **BER**. As indicated in paragraph 4.12, a calculation of the **BER** is required to be submitted to the **BCB** after completion to take account of:

a. any changes in performance between design and construction; and

b. the achieved *air permeability*, ductwork leakage and commissioned fan performance.

*The following paragraphs in this section set out what in normal circumstances would be reasonable provision to ensure that the actual performance of the building is consistent with the **BER**. The results referred to in paragraph 4.11 would assist **BCBs** in checking that the key features of the design are included as specified during the construction process.*

Building fabric

5.2 The building fabric should be constructed to a reasonable quality so that:

a. the insulation is reasonably continuous over the whole building envelope; and

b. the *air permeability* is within reasonable limits.

Continuity of insulation

5.3 The building fabric should be constructed so that there are no reasonably avoidable thermal bridges in the insulation layers caused by gaps within the various elements, at the joints between elements and at the edges of elements such as those around window and door openings.

5.4 Reductions in thermal performance can occur where the air barrier and the insulation layer are not contiguous and the cavity between them is subject to air movement. To avoid this problem, either the insulation layer should be contiguous with the air barrier at all points in the building envelope, or the space between them should be filled with solid material such as in a masonry wall.

5.5 Where calculated in support of the approaches set out in paragraph 5.7a and 5.7b, linear thermal transmittances and temperature factors should be calculated following the guidance set out in BR 497[22]. Reasonable provision would be to demonstrate

that the specified details achieve a temperature factor that is no worse than the performance set out in BRE IP 1/06[23].

5.6 Similarly, in support of the approaches set out in paragraphs 5.7a and 5.7b, the builder would have to demonstrate that an appropriate system of site inspection is in place to give confidence that the construction procedures achieve the required standards of consistency.

5.7 Ways of demonstrating that reasonable provision has been made are:

a. To adopt a quality-assured accredited construction details approach in accordance with a scheme approved by the Secretary of State. If such a scheme is utilised then the calculated linear thermal transmittance can then be used directly in the **BER** calculation;

For new buildings other than dwellings, such schemes provide independent third party checking of the calculation of linear thermal transmittance and buildability of construction details. The use of such schemes may also allow a reduction in the Building Control charges.

b. To use details that have not been subject to independent assessment of the construction method. However, in this case, the linear thermal transmittance should still have been calculated by a person with suitable expertise and experience following the guidance set out in BR 497, and a process flow sequence should be provided to the **BCB** indicating the way in which the detail should be constructed. The calculated value increased by 0.02 W/mK or 25 per cent whichever is greater, can then be used in the **BER** calculation.

*Evidence of suitable expertise and experience for calculating linear thermal transmittance would be to demonstrate that the person has been trained in the software used to carry out the calculation, has applied that model to the example calculations set out in BR 497 and has achieved results that are within the stated tolerances. Builders following this route will inevitably add to the burden of checking required of the **BCB** and adopting this route may attract higher building control fees than the alternative approaches.*

c. To use unaccredited details, with no specific quantification of the thermal bridge values. In such cases, the generic linear thermal bridge values as given in IP 1/06 increased by 0.04 W/mK or 50 per cent whichever is greater must be used in the **BER** calculation.

---

[22] BR 497 *Conventions for calculating linear thermal transmittance and temperature factors*, BRE 2007.

[23] IP 1/06 *Assessing the effects of thermal bridging at junctions and around openings in the external elements of buildings*, BRE, 2006.

5.8	The alternative approaches (a) and (b) above are not mutually exclusive. For example, a builder could use the accredited construction details scheme approach for the majority of the junctions, but use a bespoke detail for the window head. In this case, the 0.02 W/mK or 25 per cent whichever is greater margin would apply only to the thermal transmittance of the window head detail.

Air permeability and pressure testing

5.9	In order to demonstrate that an acceptable *air permeability* has been achieved, Regulation 20B states:

20B.–(1) This regulation applies to the erection of a building in relation to which paragraph L1(a)(i) of Schedule 1 imposes a requirement.

(2) Where this regulation applies, the person carrying out the work shall, for the purpose of ensuring compliance with regulation 17C and paragraph L1(a)(i) of Schedule 1:

a.	ensure that:

  i.	pressure testing is carried out in such circumstances as are approved by the Secretary of State; and

  ii.	the testing is carried out in accordance with a procedure approved by the Secretary of State; and

b.	subject to paragraph (5), give notice of the results of the testing to the local authority.

(3) The notice referred to in paragraph (2)(b) shall:

a.	record the results and the data upon which they are based in a manner approved by the Secretary of State; and

b.	be given to the local authority not later than seven days after the final test is carried out.

(4) A local authority is authorised to accept, as evidence that the requirements of paragraph (2)(a)(ii) have been satisfied, a certificate to that effect by a person who is registered by the British Institute of Non-destructive Testing in respect of pressure testing for the air tightness of buildings.

(5) Where such a certificate contains the information required by paragraph (3)(a), paragraph (2)(b) does not apply.

5.10	The approved procedure for pressure testing is given in the ATTMA publication *Measuring air permeability of building envelopes*[24] and, specifically, the method that tests the building envelope. The preferred test method is that trickle ventilators should be temporarily sealed rather than just closed. *BCB*s should be provided with evidence that test equipment has been calibrated within the previous 12 months using a UKAS-accredited facility. The manner approved for recording the results and the data on which they are based is given in section 4 of that document.

5.11	*BCBs* are authorised to accept, as evidence of compliance, a certificate offered under regulation 20B(4). It should be confirmed to the *BCB* that the person has received appropriate training and is registered to test the specific class of building concerned.

5.12	The approved circumstances under which the Secretary of State requires pressure testing to be carried out are set out in paragraphs 5.13 to 5.18.

5.13	All buildings that are not *dwellings* (including extensions which are being treated as new buildings for the purposes of complying with Part L) must be subject to pressure testing, with the following exceptions:

a.	Buildings less than 500 m² **total useful floor area**; in this case the developer may choose to avoid the need for a pressure test provided that the *air permeability* used in the calculation of the *BER* is taken as 15 m³/(h.m²) at 50 Pa.

Compensating improvements in other elements of the building fabric and building services will be needed to keep the BER no worse than the TER.

b.	A factory-made modular building of less than 500 m² floor area, with a planned time of use of more than 2 years at more than one location, and where no site assembly work is needed other than making linkages between standard modules using standard link details. Compliance with regulation 20B can be demonstrated by giving a notice to the local authority confirming that the building as installed conforms to one of the standard configurations of modules and link details for which the installer has pressure test data from a minimum of five in-situ measurements incorporating the same module types and link details as utilised in the actual building. The results must indicate that the average test result is better than the *design air permeability* as specified in the *BER* calculation by not less than 1.0 m³/(h.m²) at 50 Pa.

c.	Large extensions (whose compliance with Part L is being assessed as if they were new buildings – see Approved Document L2B) where sealing off the extension from the existing building is impractical. The ATTMA publication gives guidance both on how extensions can be tested and on situations where pressure tests are inappropriate. Where it is agreed with the *BCB* that testing is impractical, the extension should be treated as a large, complex building, with the guidance in paragraph 5.13d applying.

---

[24]	*Measuring air permeability of building envelopes*, Technical Standard L2, ATTMA, 2010.

d. Large complex buildings, where due to building size or complexity it may be impractical to carry out pressure testing of the whole building. The ATTMA publication indicates those situations where such considerations might apply. Before adopting this approach developers must produce in advance of construction work in accordance with the approved procedure a detailed justification of why pressure testing is impractical. This should be endorsed by a suitably qualified person such as a competent person approved for pressure testing. In such cases, a way of showing compliance would be to appoint a suitably qualified person to undertake a detailed programme of design development, component testing and site supervision to give confidence that a continuous air barrier will be achieved. It would not be reasonable to claim **air permeability** better than 5.0 m³/(h.m²) at 50 Pa has been achieved.

One example of a suitably qualified person would be an ATTMA member. The 5.0 m³/(h.m²) at 50 Pa limit has been set because at better standards the actual level of performance becomes too vulnerable to single point defects in the air barrier.

e. Compartmentalised buildings: where buildings are compartmentalised into self-contained units with no internal connections it may be impractical to carry out whole building pressure tests. In such cases reasonable provision would be to carry out a pressure test on a representative area of the building as detailed in the ATTMA guidance. In the event of a test failure, the provisions of paragraphs 5.14 and 5.15 would apply, but it would be reasonable to carry out a further test on another representative area to confirm that the expected standard is achieved in all parts of the building.

5.14   Compliance with the requirement in Paragraph L1(a)(i) would be demonstrated if:

a. the measured **air permeability** is not worse than the limiting value of 10 m³/(h.m²) at 50 Pa; and

b. the **BER** calculated using the measured **air permeability** is not worse than the **TER**.

*If it proves impractical to meet the **design air permeability**, any shortfall must be compensated through improvements to subsequent fit-out activities. Builders may therefore wish to schedule pressure tests early enough to facilitate remedial work on the building fabric, e.g. before false ceilings are up.*

Consequences of failing a pressure test

5.15   If satisfactory performance is not achieved, then remedial measures should be carried out on the building and new tests carried out until the building achieves the criteria set out in paragraph 5.14.

*If the measured **air permeability** on retest is greater than the **design air permeability** but less than the limiting value of 10 m³/(h.m²) then other improvements may be required to achieve the **TER**. This means that builders would be unwise to claim a **design air permeability** better than 10 unless they are confident of achieving the improved value.*

COMMISSIONING OF THE BUILDING SERVICES SYSTEMS

5.16   Paragraph L1(b)(iii) of Schedule 1 to the Building Regulations requires **fixed building services** to be commissioned by testing and adjustment as necessary to ensure that they use no more fuel and power than is reasonable in the circumstances. In order to demonstrate that the heating and hot water systems have been adequately commissioned, regulation 20C states:

20C Commissioning

(A1) This regulation applies to building work in relation to which paragraph F1(2) of Schedule 1 imposes a requirement, but does not apply to the provision or extension of any fixed system for mechanical ventilation or any associated controls where testing and adjustment is not possible.

(1) This regulation applies to building work in relation to which paragraph L1(b) of Schedule 1 imposes a requirement, but does not apply to the provision or extension of any fixed building service where testing and adjustment is not possible or would not affect the energy efficiency of that fixed building service.

(2) Where this regulation applies the person carrying out the work shall, for the purpose of ensuring compliance with paragraph F1(2) or L1(b) of Schedule 1, give to the local authority a notice confirming that the fixed building services have been commissioned in accordance with a procedure approved by the Secretary of State.

(3) The notice shall be given to the local authority–

a. not later than the date on which the notice required by regulation 15(4) is required to be given; or

b. where that regulation does not apply, not more than 30 days after completion of the work.

5.17   It would be useful to prepare a **commissioning** plan, identifying the systems that need to be tested and the tests that will be carried out and provide this with the design-stage **TER/BER** calculation so that the **BCB** can check that the **commissioning** is being done as the work proceeds.

The use of the templates in the Model Commissioning Plan (BSRIA BG 8/2009) is a way of documenting the process in an appropriate way.

5.18 Not all *fixed building services* will need to be commissioned. With some systems it is not possible as the only controls are 'on' and 'off' switches. Examples of this would be some mechanical ventilation systems or single fixed electrical heaters. In other cases *commissioning* would be possible but in the specific circumstances would have no effect on energy use.

5.19 Where *commissioning* is carried out it must be done in accordance with procedures approved by the Secretary of State comprising:

a. the CIBSE Commissioning Code M: *Commissioning management*[25]; and

This provides guidance on the overall process and includes a schedule of all the relevant guidance documents relating to the **commissioning** *of specific building services systems.*

b. the procedures for leakage testing of ductwork given in paragraphs 5.27 and 5.28.

5.20 *Commissioning* must be carried out in such a way as not to prejudice compliance with any applicable health and safety requirements.

5.21 *Commissioning* is often carried out by the person who installs the system. Sometimes it may be carried out by a subcontractor or even by a specialist firm. It is important that whoever carries it out follows the relevant approved procedure.

Notice of Completion

5.22 The Building Regulations (regulation 20C(2)) and the Building (Approved Inspectors etc) Regulations (regulation 12C(2)) require that a notice be given to the relevant **BCB** that **commissioning** has been carried out according to a procedure approved by the Secretary of State.

5.23 The notice should include a declaration confirming that:

a. a *commissioning* plan has been followed so that every system has been inspected and commissioned in an appropriate sequence and to a reasonable standard; and

b. the results of tests confirm that the performance is reasonably in accordance with the actual building design, including written commentaries where excursions are proposed to be accepted.

It would be helpful to **BCBs** *if such declarations were to be signed by someone suitably qualified by relevant training and experience. A way of achieving this would be to employ a member of the Commissioning Specialists Association or the Commissioning Group of the HVCA in respect of HVAC systems, or a member of the Lighting Industry Commissioning Scheme in respect of fixed internal or external lighting. The use of the templates in the Model Commissioning Plan[26] is a way of documenting the process in an appropriate way.*

5.24 Where a building notice or full plans have been given to a local authority, the notice should be given within 5 days of the completion of the *commissioning* work; in other cases, for example where work is carried out by a person registered with a competent person scheme (see paragraphs 3.13 to 3.17), it must be given within 30 days.

5.25 Where an approved inspector is the **BCB**, the notice should generally be given within 5 days of the completion of the *commissioning* work. However, where the work is carried out by a person registered with a competent person scheme (see paragraphs 3.13 to 3.17) the notice must be given within 30 days. Where the installation of *fixed building services* which require *commissioning* is carried out by a person registered with a competent person scheme the notice of *commissioning* will be given by that person.

5.26 Until the **BCB** receives the commissioning notice it may not be able to be reasonably satisfied that Part L has been complied with and consequently is unlikely to be able to give a completion/ final certificate.

Air leakage testing of ductwork

5.27 Ductwork leakage testing should be carried out in accordance with the procedures set out in HVCA DW/143[27] on systems served by fans with a design flow rate greater than 1 m^3/s and for those sections of ductwork where:

a. the pressure class is such that DW/143 recommends testing; or

b. the **BER** calculation assumes a leakage rate for a given section of ductwork that is better than the standard for its particular pressure class. In such cases, any low-pressure ductwork should be tested using the DW/143 testing provisions for medium-pressure ductwork. The pressure classes are set out in Table 5.

DW/143 does not call for any testing of low-pressure ductwork. However, where the builder is claiming that the low-pressure ductwork will be less leaky than the normal low-pressure class allowance to achieve an improved **BER***, this better standard should be demonstrated by testing using the procedures set out for medium-pressure ductwork.*

Membership of the HVCA specialist ductwork group or the Association of Ductwork Contractors and Allied Services could be a way of demonstrating suitable qualifications for this testing work.

---

[25] CIBSE Code M: *Commissioning management*, CIBSE, 2003.
[26] BG 8/2009, *Model commissioning plan*, BSRIA, 2009

[27] DW/143 *A Practical Guide to Ductwork Leakage Testing*, HVCA, 2000.

Table 5 **Ductwork pressure classes**

Pressure class	Design static pressure (Pa)		Maximum air velocity (m/s)	Air leakage limit (l/(s.m²) of duct surface area)
	Maximum positive	Maximum negative		
Low pressure (class A)	500	500	10	$0.027\ \Delta P^{0.65}$
Medium pressure (class B)	1000	750	20	$0.009\ \Delta P^{0.65}$
High pressure (class C)	2000	750	40	$0.003\ \Delta P^{0.65}$

5.28   If a ductwork system fails to meet the leakage standard, remedial work should be carried out as necessary to achieve satisfactory performance in retests and further ductwork sections should be tested as set out in DW/143.

Section 6: Providing information

6.1 In accordance with paragraph L1(c) of Schedule 1, the owner of the building should be provided with sufficient information about the building, the **fixed building services** and their maintenance requirements so that the building can be operated in such a manner as to use no more fuel and power than is reasonable in the circumstances.

Building log book

6.2 A way of showing compliance with the requirement would be to produce information following the guidance in CIBSE TM 31 *Building log book toolkit*[28]. The information should be presented in templates as or similar to those in the TM. The information could draw on or refer to information available as part of other documentation, such as the Operation and Maintenance Manuals and the Health and Safety file required by the CDM Regulations.

6.3 The data used to calculate the **TER** and the **BER** should be included with the log book. The occupier should also be provided with the recommendations report generated in parallel with the 'on-construction' Energy Performance Certificate. This will inform the occupier how the energy performance of the building might be further improved.

*It would also be sensible to retain an electronic copy of the **TER/BER** input file for the energy calculation to facilitate any future analysis that may be required by the owner when altering or improving the building.*

---

[28] TM 31 *Building log book toolkit*, CIBSE, 2006.

Section 7: Model designs

7.1   Some builders may prefer to adopt model design packages rather than to engage in design for themselves. Such model packages of fabric U-values, boiler seasonal efficiencies, window opening allowances, etc. should achieve compliant overall performance within certain constraints. The construction industry may develop model designs for this purpose and make them available on the Internet at: www.modeldesigns.info.

7.2   It will still be necessary to demonstrate compliance in the particular case by going through the procedures described in paragraphs 4.7 to 4.15.

Appendix A: Reporting evidence of compliance

1. To facilitate effective communication between the builder and **BCB**, it would be beneficial to adopt a standardised format for presenting the evidence that demonstrates compliance with the **energy efficiency requirements**. (Other than the CO_2 target which is mandatory, the compliance criteria represent reasonable provision in normal circumstances. In unusual circumstances, alternative limits may represent reasonable provision, but this would have to be demonstrated in the particular case.)

2. Since the data in compliance software and the results they calculate can provide a substantial proportion of the evidence in support of the compliance demonstration, it is anticipated that compliance software will produce this report as a standard output option.

3. It is anticipated that two versions of the standardised report would be produced by the compliance software: the first before commencement of works to include the **TER/BER** calculation plus supporting list of specifications and the second after completion to include the as built **TER/BER** calculation plus any changes to the list of specifications. The first design-stage report and accompanying list of specifications can then be used by the **BCB** to assist checking that what has been designed is actually built. A standardised report should enable the source of the evidence to be indicated, and allow the credentials of those submitting the evidence to be declared.

4. An important part of demonstrating compliance is to make a clear connection between the product specifications and the data inputs required by the compliance software (e.g. what is the wall construction that delivers the claimed U-value?). Examples as to how compliance software might provide this link are:

   a. By giving each data input a reference code that can be mapped against a separate submission by the builder/developer that details the specification corresponding to each unique reference code in the data input.

   b. By providing a fee-text entry facility along with each input parameter that has a unique reference code, thereby allowing the software to capture the specification of each item and so include the full details in an integrated output report.

   c. By including one or more utility programs that derive the data input from the specification, e.g. a U-value calculator that conforms to BR 443 and that calculates the U-value based on the layer thicknesses and conductivities, repeating thermal bridge effects etc. Outputs from such a utility program could then automatically generate the type of integrated report described at b. above.

   It would also help the **BCB** if the software included a facility to compare the 'as designed' and 'as constructed' data input files and automatically produce a schedule of changes.

5. The report should highlight any items whose specification is better than typically expected values. The **BCB** can then give particular attention to such 'key features', as their appropriate installation will be critical in achieving the **TER**. The **BCB** is advised to give particular attention to those aspects where the claimed specification delivers an energy efficiency standard in advance of that defined in the following schedule.

Wall U-value	0.23 W/m².K
Roof U-value	0.15 W/m².K
Floor U-value	0.20 W/m².K
Window/door U-value	1.5 W/m².K
Design air permeability	5.0 m³/h.m² at 50 Pa

Fixed Building Service efficiency more than 15% better than that recommended for its type in the *Non-Domestic Building Services Compliance Guide*.

Use of any low-carbon or renewable energy technology.

Appendix B: Documents referred to

Air Tightness Testing and Measurement Association (ATTMA)

www.attma.org

Measuring air permeability of building envelopes, Technical Standard L2, ATTMA 2010.

BRE

www.bre.co.uk

BR 443 Conventions for U-value calculations, 2006. (Downloadable from www.bre.co.uk/uvalues)

Information Paper IP1/06 Assessing the effects of thermal bridging at junctions and around openings in the external elements of buildings, 2006. ISBN 978 1 86081 904 9

BRE Report BR 497 Conventions for Calculating Linear Thermal Transmittance and Temperature Factors, 2007. ISBN 978 1 86081 986 5

Simplified Building Energy Model (SBEM) User manual and software (Available at www.2010ncm.bre.co.uk)

BSRIA

www.bsria.co.uk

BSRIA BG 8/2009 Model Commissioning Plan

CIBSE

www.cibse.org

CIBSE Commissioning Code M Commissioning Management, 2003. ISBN 978 1 90328 733 0

TM 31 Building Log Book Toolkit, CIBSE, 2006. ISBN 978 1 90328 771 2

TM 37 Design for improved solar shading control, 2006. ISBN 978 1 90328 757 6

TM 39 Building energy metering, 2010. ISBN 978 1 90684 611 4

TM 46 Energy benchmarks, 2008. ISBN 978 1 90328 795 8

Department for Business, Innovation and Skills

www.bis.gov.uk

Technical Standards and Regulations Directive 98/34/EC (Available at www.bis.gov.uk/policies/innovation/infrastructure/standardisation/tech-standards-directive)

Department for Energy and Climate Change (DECC)

www.decc.gov.uk

The Government's Standard Assessment Procedure for energy rating of dwellings, SAP 2009. (Available at www.bre.co.uk/sap2009)

Department for Communities and Local Government

www.communities.gov.uk

Notice of Approval of the methodology of calculation of the energy performance of buildings in England and Wales, CLG 2008.

National Calculation Methodology (NCM) modelling guide (for buildings other than dwellings in England and Wales), CLG 2010.

Implementation Stage Impact Assessment of Revisions to Parts F and L of the Building Regulations from 2010, CLG March 2010.

Planning Policy Statement Planning and Climate Change (Available to download from: www.communities.gov.uk/planningandbuilding/planning/planningpolicyguidance/planningpolicystatements/planningpolicystatements/ppsclimatechange/)

Department for Education and Skills (DfES)

www.dcsf.gov.uk/

Building Bulletin 101 Ventilation of School Buildings, School Building and Design Unit, 2005. (www.teachernet.gov.uk/iaq)

Health and Safety Executive (HSE)

www.hse.gov.uk

L24 Workplace Health, Safety and Welfare: Workplace (Health, Safety and Welfare) Regulations 1992, Approved Code of Practice and Guidance, The Health and Safety Commission, 1992. ISBN 978 0 71760 413 5

Heating and Ventilating Contractors' Association

http://www.hvca.org.uk/

DW/143 A practical guide to ductwork leakage testing, 2000. ISBN 978 0 90378 330 9

NBS (on behalf of Communities and Local Government)

www.thebuildingregs.com

Non-Domestic Building Services Compliance Guide

Legislation

SI 1991/1620 Construction Products Regulations 1991

SI 1994/3051 Construction Products (Amendment) Regulations 1994

SI 1994/3260 Electrical Equipment (Safety) Regulations 1994

Decision No 1/95 of the EC-Turkey Association Council of 22 December 1995

SI 2000/2531 The Building Regulations

SI 2000/2532 The Building (Approved Inspectors etc.) Regulations 2000

SI 2006/3418 The Electromagnetic Compatibility Regulations 2006

SI 2007/991 The Energy Performance of Buildings (Certificates and Inspections) (England and Wales) Regulations 2007

SI 2010/719 The Building and Approved Inspectors (Amendment) Regulations 2010

Appendix C: Standards referred to

BS EN ISO 13370:2007 Thermal performance of buildings. Heat transfer via the ground. Calculation methods.

BS EN 410:1998 Glass in building. Determination of luminous and solar characteristics of glazing.

BS EN 14351-1:2006 Windows and doors. Product standard, performance characteristics. Windows and external pedestrian doorsets without resistance to fire and/or smoke leakage characteristics.

Index